Let's Go Green!

An Earth-Friendly Coloring Book

Tiffany Prothero

DOVER PUBLICATIONS, INC.
Mineola, New York

Note

It is important to know the many different ways to help protect your planet. Going "green" is a way to make earth-friendly choices that are good for your health and good for the environment. In this coloring book, you will learn about recycling, planting trees, picking up litter, eating organic foods, using solar power, carpooling, and many other healthy, natural choices you can make to live an environmentally friendly lifestyle.

Are you ready? Let's go green!

Bibliographical Note

Let's Go Green! An Earth-Friendly Coloring Book is a new work, first published by Dover Publications, Inc., in 2009.

DOVER *Pictorial Archive* SERIES

International Standard Book Number
ISBN-13: 978-0-486-46817-4
ISBN-10: 0-486-46817-8

Manufactured in the United States by Courier Corporation
46817803
www.doverpublications.com

Keep your parks clean!

Support free-range farms.

Plant a tree.

Share a ride to reduce emissions.

Help keep your beaches clean.

Riding a bike will help to reduce emissions too!

Do little things to save water. Turn off the faucet while brushing your teeth.

SOLAR

ELECTRICAL PANEL

WELCOME

Using solar power in your house is more energy efficient.

PANELS

CHARGE CONTROLLER

INVERTER

BATTERY

Buy local organic foods instead of conventional foods.

Try farming on your own and grow your own tomato garden.

Learn more about wind power.

Help reduce litter by taking a reusable shopping bag to the grocery store.

Save energy by turning off the lights when they are not in use.

Ride a bus to reduce emissions.

Donate to charities.

Save for green charities.

Drying clothes outside saves energy.

Recycle!

Change your regular light bulbs to compact fluorescent light bulbs.

Help to save endangered species like the bald eagle.

Maybe you can be the person to discover the formula
for hydrogen-powered cars!

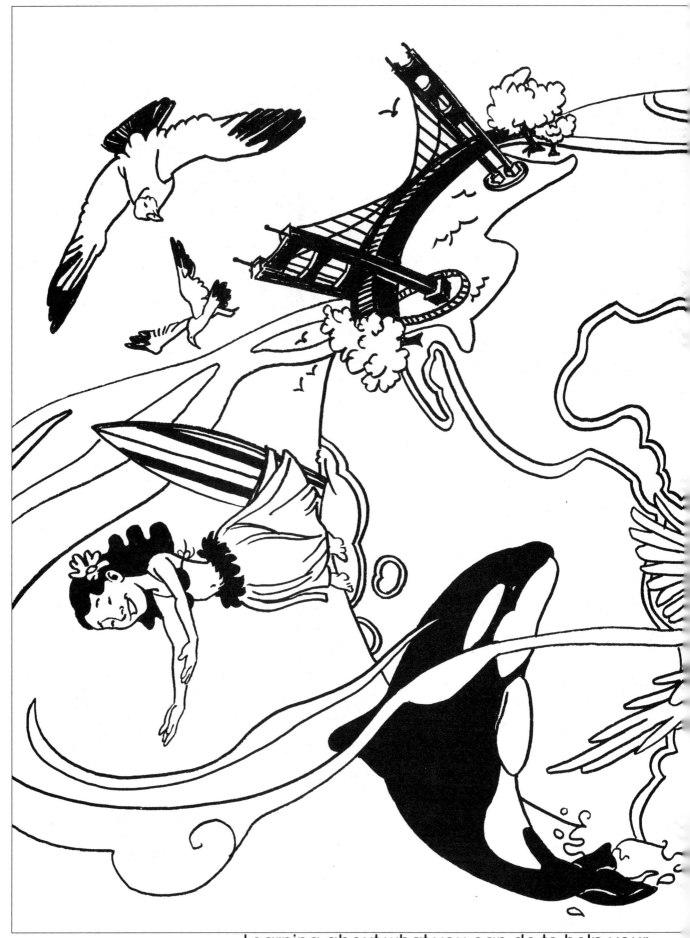

Learning about what you can do to help your

environment will lead to a clean and healthy earth.

Recycle your paper products and share.